KODAK BLACK

*

*

*

Flying High to Success

*

*

*

Weird and Interesting Facts on Dieuson Octave!

By Bern Bolo

Table Of Contents

***

Introduction

Hey, watssup homie? *ahem ahem* I mean, hello and welcome once again here at Trivia Land! I'm sorry about earlier, I was just reading so much about our artist of the day.

I think you can guess, with what I have said above, the nationality of our artist today or race. Not that I'm being racist or stereotypical or anything, but I have the feeling that he have said that at least once in his life.

So yeah, he's a black American. I believe most of them in the music industry are famous for their ballads or raps. So which one do you think he is? Any guesses? Come on, guess!

Another clue? I didn't know we're playing the guessing game, oh well. He will be turning 20 this coming June, so a late-teen black American rapper. I think there's not so abundant of them but he is one. Can you guess?

Alright here it goes, our artist of the day called by the name Kodak Black.

I know, I know, his first name sounds like, from a brand of camera or a species of a bear but it seems unique and one of a kind. And his last name is a very common name. The result was very contrasting all in all yet it still easy to remember.

So lets head-on to the life of Kodak Black!

Where I Came From

Dieuson Octave is thy name, I mean Kodak Black's real name. He was born last 11th of June 1997. His parents were immigrants from Haiti and his mother raised him in a public housing project called "Golden Acres" in Pompano Beach, Florida. The place of his birth, Pompano, has the largest percent of immigrants, Haitian immigrants, in all of the United States.

At a very young age, Dieuson is one of the victim of his environment. As you have known racism and ethnic discrimination was rampant in the United States, this makes the life of those with different race, skin color, and etc., hard! Even now, there are still some lingering prejudices even though the majority is already over.

Dieuson, being a black American, experience this kind of life. Brawling with the "Whites" became a regular thing, being exposed to drugs was ok, and getting arrested like it was expected. But not all things in his life were bad.

Dieuson started singing (or rapping really) in his elementary years.

He and his 'homeboys' also known as his cousins got interested in rap and would do it in school against older boys. In a video titled *Preude*, Dieuson's mother revealed that he was getting in trouble for rapping in class. When she asked if he will focus more on his school or his raps, his only answer was "music is his life".

At the age of 12, some older boys recognized him and what his raps. They invited him to go with them to record some of his raps.

He found out later that their place was a trap place. For those who don't know what it means, it a place where illegal drugs are sold. At first, he was skeptical since some of the boys were doing or selling drugs but he still went every day to rap. Later on, he adopted and felt like a second home to him. This little crew baptized him with a nickname "Lil Black". He was already known in the neighborhood as "Black" and was the youngest of them all.

When Black reached high school, he studied at Blanche Ely High School and joined "Brutal Yungenz", a local rap group. "Lil Black" was changed to "J-Black", which was his first official stage name. He was the youngest of the group yet he helped them gain recognition to some of their tracks like "What U Talking Bout" and "Walk With Me".

He later joined another group called "The Kolyons". They're a popular local group from Broward County. Black also started putting songs on YouTube when the group disbanded. His first song on the channel was "Diary of a Brutal Kid". "Kodak Black" is made when he used it as an Instagram username and it just got stuck.

I Got Lucky (or Talent)

The life of crime still hangs upon Black as he grows up. As his mother was the sole provider in their family, he learned another way to survive. He started robbing, which made him have several run-ins with the law, in order to help provide to his family.

At the age of 15, he was already put into Juvenile Hall three times the same year. Then on December 2013, Black got a Punishable by Life charge. He thought he was going to be in prison for his whole life or he was going to be exiled for good.

Luck, it seems, finally shines down on him. Black got the attention of A.D. Julien, CEO of Dollaz N Deaz. He believed that Black have a talent to be a star. A.D. betted on that and helped him got a lighter sentence which was probation for three years. Black, then, signed for a solo career in DND label.

At the same month (more specifically 26th of December 2013), Black was able to release his first mixtape "Project Baby". The mixtape features 18 songs that are produced by DJ Jay-R, K.E. On the Track and Rooq to name a few.

This gained him a nationwide exposure and motivation to try harder and to do better. This was a whole new level than recording in a trap house and it's the biggest opportunity he had since he started rapping.

Last October 2015, Black signed a record deal with Atlantic Records. This was at the same month Drake posted his Instagram video dancing to the song "SKRT". The single also snatched the #10 on *Billboard's* "Bubbling Under R&B/Hip-Hop Singles" chart last August 2016.

Now, I'm skeptical to comment if it's Black's or Drake's influence that makes it so successful. Not that the song is not good, just not my cup of tea. It was a so-so for me. Everyone around the world think otherwise.

The Path Have Already Been Paved

From being arrested to having a bright future in the music industry was the fate Kodak Black had at 15 years old. He knew that he's talented but never to actually have the opportunity until opportunity knocks unexpectedly - Opportunity really does knock at unexpected times.

Black immediately dropped his first mixtape "Project Baby". "Heart of The Projects", was his second mixtape, which was released on 30th of December 2014. This gains a whole new attention since Drake, a Canadian rapper, co-signed with him for Black's "SKRT". In his *Prelude* video, he says that he knows about it but didn't know nor care what it did. His nonchalance of it all is amazing since Drake was already a well-known artist.

Exactly a year after Black's second mixtape (December 2015), he released another mixtape entitled "Institution". This 24 track set help him solidify his reputation outside his hometown. He revealed to an interview with *XXL* that he came up with the name while being detained in Virginia. He also says that *Institution* was what you do or wake up for every day.

Quite fitting, if you ask me. The institution also means an established official organization having an important role in the life of a country. He had run-ins with the law since he was young and he named that mixtape when he was arrested. Ironic!

French Montana, an American rapper, released a single titled "Lockjaw" on 27ᵗʰ of May 2016. Kodak black was featured on this single which was also from Montana's mixtape "MC4". It took the place of #23 on *Billboard's* Hot R&B/Hip-Hop Songs chart.

"Lil B.I.G. Pac" was the most successful out of all his records. The 13 track mixtape was released on 11ᵗʰ of June 2016 and was produced by the like of Honorable C.N.O.T.E and J-Gramm. There were guest appearances as well. PnB Rock and Gucci Mane are some of the examples. "Lil B.I.G. Pac" snagged #18 and # 48 of the Heatseekers Albums and Top R&B/Hip-Hop Albums charts, respectively. This was also Black's first record to reach the Billboard charts, which make the greatest birthday gift for him.

At the same month, XXL's 2016 Freshman Class" included our artist of the day. The segment of the magazine told all the readers all the unknown artist-to-watch that are considered to rise. They usually appeared on the front cover of the magazine, which Black did with 9 other upcoming artists.

The "Tunnel Vision" was the very first one to reach the top 10 on the *Billboard's* Hot 100 chart, it peaked to #6 and #17 on Canadian Hot 100. The was released last 17ᵗʰ of February 2017 and is included in his debut studio album, *Painting Pictures* that was released last 31ˢᵗ of March.

At the same month, "Tunnel Vision", together with "No Flockin" from *Heart of the Projects*, got an acknowledgment from Recording Industry Association of America (RIAA) as a certified Gold Record.

This Is The Real Me

"Real could be anything as long as you're solid." This was Kodak Black's comment on an interview with *Passion of The Weiss.*

Every artist has their own unique way in presenting their music. For the Pompano rapper, his music is his way to express his life. Most, if not all, of his songs, reflect what is happening to him or around him. That kind of artist is one of my favorite. If there song is about life challenges, I would love it. Emotions and authenticity of the situations are the most important tool in creating music.

Black also has an opinion on those rappers who "are just talking rubbish". He doesn't want to become like them. They don't know what they're talking about. The only thing they rap at is so immature.

But he doesn't judge them if they present themselves as such. He would know if they were genuine by how they talk, how they walk, how and what they wear. Well, the first impression is really your base of everything and the music they write is the in-depth of them.

Black, himself, admitted that his music was mostly influenced by 'Lil Boosie', Chief Keef and it present most of his misdeeds in law. He also portrays on his songs all the things he observed that's happening around him.

An article in *The New Yorker* mentioned that Black doesn't follow how rap was written before. The elements of individualism, personal venting and the variety of putting the lyrics are missing.

It was followed by an article in *The Fader*. It says he resembled Mobb Deep and Lil' Wayne, a young artist of the 90's. All of them put their intelligent, equally emotional, observation of their life and those around them. This makes it more genuine since he wasn't the only one to experience it. Black knows that there were others who could relate like his fans.

The Legalities Of It All

For Kodak Black, Music and Crime seem to be Back-on-Back on his life. I have read the start of his career, Black got a Punishable By Life charge at 15 and got away with three-year probation and a record deal.

He had been a 'good boy' for several months. He was writing raps and releasing note-worthy singles. But the life of crime seems to like him too much to let him go.

Last October 2015, Black was arrested for possession of cannabis and driving with suspended license. He was originally stopped for a traffic violation but was found with a small quantity of weed, resulting a suspension of his license and outstanding charges; assault, kidnapping and robbery, which he got out of with a $1,000 bail.

On the same month, he was approached by Atlantic Records for a record deal, which he signed by the way. Such a good fortune seems to lands on his lap.

Last 2016, Black was arrested twice. First, last 21st of April, according to the detectives, Black was fleeing from the officers with a car that was said to be use in a drug deal. The chasers also mentioned that he was trying to hide a gun in a dumpster. This comes with a $5,100 bail.

While the 18th of May, he was arrested due to robbery, false imprisonment, marijuana possession and driving without a driver's license. I am thinking there is a theme on his charges. It's almost the same charges over and over again. This time he was detained in Broward County Jail.

Of course let's not forgot the good equivalent of it. He seems able to bounce back every arrest. French Montana's "Lockjaw" was released 9 days after his arrest in May and got a spot on *Billboard's* Hot R&B/Hip-Hop Songs. See! I told you. His wheel of fortune is constantly turning.

August was the time when he was about to be released (with the agreement of taking anger management class, performed the required community service, five-year probation and one-year house arrest) but behold, police found two outstanding warrants.

He was accused of sexual conduct and felony in Florence, South Carolina when he was there for his show at Treasure City nightclub. Another one was from St. Lucie County, Florida for misdemeanor cannabis possession, which he pleaded no contest in September. Black pleaded no contest on the second allegation and was credited to serve 120 days and suspension to drive for a year while he bails for the first one for $100K?

On the other side of the coin, his single "SKRT" reached top 10 of *Billboard's* "Bubbling Under R&B/Hip-Hop Singles". If I didn't know better nor was it so serious, I would say it's all publicity stunt, it looks like!. You can't also deny that this garnered so many press attentions and he was put in the public's eye.

This year (2017), Black has arrested once again in February for violating his probation. He was caught on video at a boxing match and at the Miami strip club when he wasn't supposed to. There were also allegations that he didn't complete, such as his anger management classes. He was detained and was denied to bail until his trial.

This all happen the day after he released his new single "Tunnel Vision" and "Painting Pictures" after his court trial. Coincidence or not, it still uncanny that he have his arrest and release of singles so close to each other. If it's not a publicity stunt then maybe it's the adrenaline rush or his Muse calling.

FUN Facts!

Alright, I know that most of his life is already in the public's eye. What's with his arrest and mixtape or single released so close to each other. Not to mention that he is very active on his social media, like Twitter and Instagram.

All that I could gather is the small tidbits of fact and information from our artist. I found this more eye opening to his personal life. Did you know?

Black momentarily stop writing raps but after being a charge of PBL at the age of 15 he started writing again. This was, like, an eye opener to him. I believe he said "I rather write raps and get arrest" or something along those lines.

I want to ask, have you seen the series **Orange is the New Black**? No? Well, I tell you that a character of that series named Suzanne Warren also known as "Crazy Eyes" is where Kodak Black's hairstyle came from. More like, it was inspired by that person.

He wasn't the only one to try that hairstyle as well. I think I saw Rihanna with that hairstyle once but Black make it his permanent hairstyle and believe me it looks very cool!

It's a well-known fact that Lil Boosie or professionally known as Boosie Badazz influenced Black in his music. That's not the only one he influenced. Boosie's life story of success was the reason Black want to try to go into the music industry. I believe it was the "If he can, then so can I" saying.

"So can I", he did. Black was able to write a single featuring Boosie entitled "Going Viral" on 11th of July 2016. It's amazing. Back then he was only listening to him, now he his recording with him. For me, that's the biggest achievement of life. I don't know about him . . .

Another interesting fact that I have uncovered about Black was that he played basketball and football. He was a cornerback and slot receiver. Black's reason why he likes to play defense was because he loves to tackle, to hit low at the ankles. Right now, his is playing football as a running back. That means he will need to shy away from the defense line, which was his older brother's former position. Black mentioned that he will be training him and every game will be available on Instagram if he Touchdown. That a unique way to spend time with each other.

The one that I found so emotional was when Black was the "2016 Freshman Class" of XXL magazine. His mother, when she got the issue, was squealing and shouting "Oh My God its Kodak"! Black's mother really loves him and one of his biggest supporters, she believes Kodak will get this far.

References

https://en.wikipedia.org/wiki/Kodak_Black

http://www.passionweiss.com/2014/10/01/kodak-black-project-baby-interview/

http://antidiary.com/video/watch/vid47J04jyP3eu_FmA

http://kodak-world.com/?page_id=24

http://www.aceshowbiz.com/celebrity/kodak_black/biography.html

http://www.aceshowbiz.com/celebrity/kodak_black/biography_2.html

http://www.xxlmag.com/rap-music/the-break/2016/01/the-break-presents-kodak-black/

http://www.xxlmag.com/news/2016/03/kodak-black-prelude-documentary/

http://wsvn.com/news/local/south-florida-rapper-arrested-in-hallandale-beach/

http://theboombox.com/kodak-black-arrested-robbery-kidnapping-assault-charges/

http://theboombox.com/kodak-black-arrested-again-charges-include-robbery-and-false-imprisonment/

http://www.sun-sentinel.com/news/florida/fl-reg-kodak-black-arrested-again-update-20170301-story.html

http://www.newyorker.com/magazine/2016/04/25/the-teenagers-shaping-pop

http://www.thefader.com/2016/07/20/kodak-black-lil-big-pac-essay

Kendrick Lamar

Flying High to Success, Weird and Interesting Facts on KENDRICK LAMAR DUCKWORTH

Learn all about Kendrick Lamar in 20 minutes
With **Bern Bolo**
The Bathroom Genius

I am pretty sure, you know him very well. He has collaborated with a lot of iconic people, legendary music and rap icons like Dr. Dre (yes… BEATS by DRE - yup), Lil Wayne and more! His songs are amazing, his raps and lyrics are superb!

"Get the f*ck off my stage, I'm the Sandman.
Get the f*ck off my d*ck, that ain't right
I make a play f*cking up your whole life!

If I kill a <u>nigga</u>, it <u>won't be</u> the alcohol, <u>ayy</u>
I'm the <u>realest nigga </u>after all, bitch, be humble!"

Soooo……

Bitch Sit Down And Be HUMBLE!!!

As for Kendrick Lamar's fans like me, I only do not like the message of the song but I also love the video – keeps playing over and over and over again…Did you know that he saw his first murder at age five? Ooohhh… certainly, what a bad and awful way for someone to die – and definitely what a gruesome way for a child like him at that time to have witnessed. *Imagine the horror….!* Now we could again say that this is yet another sad story to tell about our featured artist. Well, it is just definitely a good thing to know that he had overcome all of these and look at where he is now! And yet, he stays HUMBLE. *Way to go Lamar!* He is the one, the only, the new rising king of rap – molded by Dr. Dre himself and from the streets of Compton… Mr. Kendrick Lamar Duckworth! Now if you are quite interested in him, knowing about his life, or maybe you just wanna get over with the boredom you're feeling, then you came to the perfect place. Tell your friends about Kendrick Lamar too and give this creation a GO!

Check Out Kendrick Lamar's Trivia
Get your copy of Kendrick Lamar's Trivia!

If you enjoyed this "Trivia", please leave an honest review on Amazon.com!

Sign-up here on Bern Bolo's site for Trivia On Twenty One Pilots!